So I Said

So I Said

Quotes and Thoughts
of Gerry Spence

Gerry Spence

LARGE PRINT EDITION

Sastrugi Press

Jackson Hole

Sastrugi Press / Published by arrangement with the author
So I Said: Quotes and Thoughts of Gerry Spence
www.sastrugipress.com
Library of Congress Catalog-in-Publication Data
Library of Congress Control Number: 2018934302
Spence, Gerry
So I Said / Gerry Spence - 1st United States edition
p. cm.
1. Quotations, English 2. Motivation—maxims, etc. 3. Inspiration
Summary: This collection of forty years of quotes and thoughts by trial lawyer Gerry Spence are for provoking thought and discussion.

ISBN-13: 978-1-944986-37-7 (hardback)
ISBN-13: 978-1-944986-38-4 (paperback)
ISBN-13: 978-1-64922-130-8 (hardback large print)
ISBN-31: 978-1-64922-131-5 (paperback large print)
818-dc22
Printed in the United States of America when purchased in the United States
10 9 8 7 6 5 4 3 2 1

Table of Contents

Introduction

Have you ever had a conversation with a lost butterfly?

This book is a collection of sayings by Gerry Spence, the famous trial lawyer. It's about the ins-and-outs of life—about living and loving and struggling and dying, and it's presented in short, pithy adages that Spence has authored over the years and that have been borrowed from his many works. And some just fluttered down out of the blue like a lost butterfly.

Spence is an old man. He was old before most of you were born, and he's still hanging around at eighty-nine. If an old man is lucky, the words that escape his weathered lips make sense. If they make sense, someone might claim that his words are wise, or clever, or revealing, or one might respond, "I never thought of that," which doesn't mean what was said was prophetic or judicious or even relevant. Jesus said, "Love one another." Simple. A perfect way of life in three words. But it appears that one has to be crucified in order for such words to become immortal. Crucifixion, we're told, is not a part of Spence's life plan.

So who is this old man who offers up this book of his sayings? Why should we listen to him? What has he done? Is he famous? Or is he some toothless old wretch sitting on a curb somewhere jabbering into the air? Good questions. In truth, wisdom can be gleaned from any source if we are wise enough to catch it, chew it, and digest it.

For most of his life, Spence has been a trial lawyer fighting in our courts across the land for people—*only* people—mostly the poor, the lost, the forgotten, and the damned. Yes, he's represented the famous and the wealthy, including Imelda Marcos, the First Lady of the Philippines, and Geoffrey Fieger, the Michigan guru of the bar and others—but his wife, Imaging, says that those who enjoy high positions sometimes need more help than the poor because the privileged and the powerful usually have had less experience in the art of suffering.

Spence was born, reared, and educated in Wyoming. He graduated *cum laude* from the University of Wyoming Law School in 1952. He's spent most of his life in court and has tried and won many celebrated cases.

In 2009, Spence was inducted into the American Trial Lawyers Hall of Fame, which includes John Adams and Clarence Darrow. One can see those two last-mentioned old boys pushing up out of their graves, raising their eyebrows and pointing at Spence and asking, "Who? Him? Why him?"

Along the way, the University of Wyoming, Spence's alma mater, presented Spence with an Honorary Doctor of Law degree. He was awarded the first Lifetime Achievement Award from the Consumer Attorneys of California (formerly California Trial Lawyers Association), and the Golden Plate Award for Law and Literature by the American Academy of Achievement, and many others.

In 1979, he successfully defended Ed Cantrell, the chief law enforcement officer in Rock Springs, Wyoming, on a murder charge. Cantrell shot his own undercover deputy between the eyes as they faced each other—Cantrell, the fastest gun in the West, pulling down on Deputy Michael Rosa to beat him to the draw. It was a big media case.

In 1981, a federal jury in Cheyenne awarded Kimberly Pring, the former Miss Wyoming, $26.5 million against "Penthouse Magazine" for their libel, then (and perhaps now) the largest libel verdict in the nation's history.

His case against Kerr-McGee, the Oklahoma chemical company, surrounding the mysterious death of Karen Silkwood, first brought him to national attention with a $10 million punitive award against that company, at that time the largest damage award of its kind. Silkwood was portrayed by Meryl Streep in the movie *Silkwood*. The 1983 film was nominated for a variety of Academy Awards.

In 1990, after a three-month trial in New York City, Spence defended the First Lady of the Philippines, Imelda Marcos, charged with racketeering and fraud for allegedly stealing more than $200 million from the Philippine Treasury. A jury acquitted her on all counts.

In the 1992 case of the famous standoff at Ruby Ridge, government agents shot and killed Sammy Weaver in the back while he was running home. He was fourteen years old. Then the government shot and killed his mother, Vicki Weaver, and eventually shot and wounded Randy Weaver, his father, as well as a family friend, Kevin Harris. When Weaver finally surrendered, he was charged with multiple crimes. Spence successfully defended Weaver on a wrongful murder charge of a federal agent. Spence's defense rested on cross-examination of the government witnesses, without calling a single witness of his own. The government later paid damages to the Weaver family for its wrongdoing.

In 2008, in a politically charged case brought by the Justice Department in Michigan against the famous attorney Geoffrey Fieger, Spence won complete acquittals for Mr. Fieger on a ten-count indictment alleging federal campaign contribution violations, conspiracy, and obstruction of justice.

He has tried and won numerous other well-known murder and civil cases. Some of his cases have been reversed on appeal by various courts of appeal. Others settled. But Spence's record of jury verdicts in civil cases and acquittals in criminal cases, without an intervening loss, is unmatched in the annals of jury trials.

Spence has never lost a criminal case either as a prosecutor or as a defense attorney. He's not lost a civil case since 1969. He's won more multi-million dollar verdicts for people without an intervening loss than any lawyer in America.

Spence is the founder of the Trial Lawyer's College, which teaches both civil and criminal lawyers how to represent the people, the ordinary citizen, against the massive power of corporate America.

Spence is the author of seventeen other books including the best selling *How to Argue and Win Every Time* and the widely acclaimed novel *Half Moon and Empty Stars*. He lives in Jackson Hole, Wyoming, with his wife of nearly half a century, Imaging. They have six children and thirteen grandchildren.

Why did we put this book together? We believe you'll find some sayings here that will inspire. You may even have a good time. You may learn something. You may find something to argue about with us. You may want your money back. But, please, don't ask. Spence has six kids and countless grandkids (maybe thirteen) who might enjoy this work, too.

Preface

Over the years I've said many things in many places. These so-called "Spence-isms," this menagerie of personal axioms and quotes, originated from both my published and unpublished books and some just fluttered down out of the blue like lost butterflies.

I've learned a good deal about myself from their collection. I maintain a vital hope that some will be of interest to you, that some might even cause a smile, or a "Yeah, I know what you mean."

I discovered I have not always been consistent when gathering these. One of the freedoms I've demanded for myself is the right to contradict myself. I claim personal growth as an excuse.

These sayings mark the tracks of my history. You may be on the same trail. Or you may have taken another. In either event, I invite you to come along and see where I've been, and where we may be going.

I'm delighted you've read this far. Let's go the rest of the way together.

—*Gerry Spence*

How We Are

~

We have laws that prevent us from
throwing empty bottles on the streets
but none to keep us from throwing the
lost and the helpless there.

~

How We Are

~

We are the sum of the choices we make.

Old brains are not to be trusted. They are full of holes and have grown dusty in the corner, and refuse a decent cleaning.

Matters of the Mind

~

I would rather have a mind opened by
wonder than closed by belief.

Believing and doubting—the world is
filled with either believers who have no
proof, or doubters, who, having proof,
disbelieve the same.

~

Matters of the Mind

~

Insanity is simply the elimination of all of the mind's fences.

The most deadly trap
      —the brainwashed mind.

~

Matters of the Mind

~

Death is only a state of mind.

Hate and violence are a nasty married couple that ironically are in love.

‿

Matters of the Mind

~

Jealousy and hate are fraternal twins and adore each other's company.

Vulnerability is a state of mind.

Matters of the Mind

~

Ideas are like many marriages. Too few prove to be good, but once you're in one it's hard to get out.

Dreams are the fodder of change.

~

Matters of the Earth

~

Ownership of the Earth—the Earth does not belong to us. We belong to it.

The original music was the wind. The earliest painters were lichen.

~

Matters of the Earth

The rights of nature—trees, rocks, dandelions and creeks and all creatures, the mountains and prairies and living forests—as we, all have rights. By reason of their being, they have rights.

Matters of the Earth

~

The ultimate mother is Mother Earth. She provides us freedom, even our freedom to injure and destroy her. When we abuse her, she leaves us to learn our lessons and has provided us the intelligence to do so. She does not preach. She absorbs our negligence and abuse and greed with patience. She has never given up on us. She just loves us. We'd better love her back before, a little at a time, we become successful in finally killing our own mother.

~

Power

~

Power, like the reproductive muscle, longs
to be exercised, often without judgment
or right.

Violence, deceit, and money are the ugly
triplets of political power.

〜

Power

~

The weakness of power is that it never bargains with the powerless.

The system is the progeny of power and money and is blindly faithful to its parents.

~

Power

~

A risk-free experiment: women taking over the sole leadership of the world for the next ten thousand years, given the miserable record men have established as leaders throughout their dismal history of power.

~

Power

~

We are defined by how we use our power.

Hypocrisy is a perk of power.

∽

Power

~

All territorial conquests are generated by the power of the testosterone-laden male who follows the compass of his penis.

Power never learns.

Power

~

Testosterone is the ultimate weapon of mass destruction.

Power

~

Revenge is the bastard child of justice.

Justice is but a divine mist.

Power

~

Good citizens are often like a herd of steers waiting to be fattened and sent to the market.

Violence and its threat are the prison guards of political power.

~

Justice and Judges

~

Justice is what people in power say it is.

Justice is a dead word perfumed by sentiment.

~

Justice and Judges

~

Despite the fact that its function is to deliver justice, the justice system often ends up providing little more than a slamming door in the face of those who seek to enter.

Justice is just a word that jabs the heart, and when the door of the heart is shut, the word is only an empty sound.

~

Justice and Judges

~

Winning and injustice are often unfriendly occupants in the same bed.

Justice in the courts of America is a creature that crawls on its belly like a centipede without legs.

Justice and Judges

~

Justice is a fickle illusion—a money-making argument by lawyers—a false pledge made by lying politicians—a battle cry of old, rich men who, for more profit, send young men off to die in bloody wars.

Justice and Judges

~

Justice is "pufffff."

Lady justice has an angry heart.

∾

Justice and Judges

~

Too often justice becomes the bastard progeny of lies.

The definition of justice always begins with who we are.

Justice and Judges

~

A rational search for justice should always stand in the place of power.

The conundrum is that we turn to the police to keep us safe, but we are not safe from the police.

∽

Justice and Judges

~

Our judiciary is also inhabited by many who are addicted to power. Some prance around up there on the bench dripping with self-righteous arrogance. They are the judge! Their word is the law! And all "down there" are the lowly "subjects." Power is the drug of their existence, and they cannot get enough. As most trial lawyers will agree, we endure too many judges addicted to power.

~

Justice and Judges

~

Today those in need of a competent trial lawyer often become the victims of a justice system lost in the myths of its own making.

Justice is the petulant child of truth.

Life and Living

~

Children are entitled to the greatest respect. Children are given to us as free-flying souls, but then we clip their wings like we domesticate the wild mallard. Children should become role-models for us, for they are coated with the spirit from which they came—out of the ether, clean, innocent, brimming with the delight of life, aware of the beauty of the simplest thing; a snail, a bud....

~

Life and Living

~

I know little more as an old man than as
a child—I only have different questions.

Life—that tumultuous flake of dandruff
blowing in a galactic windstorm.

∽

Life and Living

~

The only reason to hope for old age is to give our children hope to suffer the same.

We have no experience in dying. We get but one chance at it.

Life and Living

~

The relationship between Darrow and Christ: They both cared about the lost and the forgotten. They both saw our human frailty, our bent to sin, and both had a deep understanding of our need for love and forgiveness. Not only that, both were masters at manipulating a crowd—in Darrow's case, his jury. Jesus had a jury as well—one composed of his twelve disciples. They both liked women. Likely, Darrow's only suggestion to Jesus would have been that he get a haircut.

~

Life and Living

~

Better to look into the face of the enemy than stare at the ghouls of the mind that come slinking into the night.

If one is spawned in a fishbowl, how does one know the dangers of the river?

~

Life and Living

~

Enough tears eventually harden the heart.

If one lives long enough the sequences of life travel in reverse. We become babes again.

～

Life and Living

~

If man were immortal, hope would
be useless.

~

Life and Living

~

That enigmatic trap called life: You don't know where you came from, and you don't know where you're going, and you can't get out alive. And concerning this mystery: you don't know the right questions to ask.

Life and Living

~

We will not change the world. Hopefully we at least give it a small kiss as we pass by.

Creativity keeps dripping joy into my heart.

∽

Life and Living

~

Hate enjoys an eternal life and is transferred from the dead to the living like the plague.

Mothers die with their dead children.

~

Life and Living

~

Mothers will kill for their offspring, or die for them. It's the way of mothers. Mothers are beyond the law. They function under the same law as the goose that will fight off the coyote or die in her attempt. How can mothers be held to the law of man when the law of nature is always supreme?

Humor is in the giggle of the giggler. It depends on who's giggling.

~

Life and Living

~

The tree grows bent in the direction of the prevailing wind and in the calm, can never fully right itself.

Sometimes sanity gets in the way.

Life and Living

~

The smell of fresh bread is the smell of life.

Lust is the servant of the species' survival.

~

Life and Living

~

Listen to the silence.

~

Life and Living

~

One cannot see things clearly in the mind at night. It takes the eye of day, the sun on the land, to see what flourishes in the mind.

One should never fight with one's inferiors. As for one's superiors, let them win.

~

Life and Living

~

A man has finally grown up when he can listen to his son. He's returned to his infancy when he quarrels with his wife.

What I heard I have already forgotten. What I saw I still remember.

~

Life and Living

~

Human endurance is like shoe leather.
It can walk over only so much pain and
terror before the soles are worn through.

Love and an erection are often symbiotic
twins.

~

Life and Living

~

No honest love affair was ever founded on an old man's hot breath and a young woman's seductive voice pleading, "Oh, please tell me something wise."

The only way we will save mankind is by learning to care. We have to start teaching caring in school like we teach reading and math.

~

Life and Living

~

On death: Death is that blessed eternal dreamless sleep from which there is no desire to awaken. It's a state of perfect balance between need and fulfillment. One is neither awake nor asleep. One feels all and nothing. It is both the apex of glory and the essence of the void. I will enjoy being dead. Yet I will feel no pleasure. I will have no wish for anything because I have everything and, being dead, I have nothing. Death is not the opposite of life but an eternal state where life is unnecessary, indeed, not applicable. Only when the cosmological equilibrium is ever so slightly tipped does life begin to form— life, the errant child of imbalance, the bastard offspring of a once perfect union gone haywire.

~

Life and Living

~

Why do we not excel in growing old? We've had a lifetime to learn it.

She was an open book that let the wind blow the pages.

Life and Living

~

The splendor of an evening is unseen by men seeking answers.

Luck makes no promises, and if it did, luck never keeps them.

∽

Money

~

Money is a mind altering drug.

Money is the fuel of justice. Without money, the vehicle called "justice" rusts by the side of the road.

~

Money

~

Money always talks louder than the cries of the poor.

Money is the manure that fertilizes the lies of experts.

~

History

~

What was true today soon vanishes to become the ugly history of foolish men.

One cannot live freely in the present without being bound by the past.

~

History

Precedent is the law stumbling after itself century after century and never finding the truth.

Truth

~

When truth is censored, it becomes a lie.

"The truth will out," the old sage said. Truth?
A few struggle to tell it, but it cannot be
fully told. Truth is but a blister in the brain.

~

Truth

~

A lie at the heart of a case destroys the case.

There is something about the sound of the truth that often jars the ears.

Truth

~

Truth always helps make the argument.

Truth grabs hold of simple things.

~

Truth

~

It's easier to be patriotic than truthful.

Fools tell the truth. Cowards remain mute.

Truth

~

Truth-telling and profit sometimes don't mix well.

In the law, sometimes truth and death hang out together.

~

Trials, Trial Lawyers and the Law

~

The law is often an old fool wallowing in centuries of evil precedent.

The law has no ears and is blind.

~

Trials, Trial Lawyers and the Law

~

The law is too often a lie finely dressed in truth's clothing.

In a jury trial, as in life, great power is born of being a person.

~

~

The story of a case is in the heart and not the head.

Disclosure of the self creates instant credibility.

∽

Trials, Trial Lawyers and the Law

One must be on speaking terms with the true self to create credibility.

Reasonable doubt—what a toy in the play-pen of the law!

Trials, Trial Lawyers and the Law

~

Capital punishment—when the government mimics the murder of the murderer by murdering the murderer.

~

Trials, Trial Lawyers and the Law

~

Constitutional Rights—those rights that serve both the innocent and criminal alike. When such rights are wrested from the criminal they are also taken from us.

The function of the law is not to provide justice nor to preserve freedom. The function of the law is to keep those who hold power in power.

~

Trials, Trial Lawyers and the Law

~

Today trial lawyers could be as pure and honest as Jesus in a pin-striped suit—and still the jurors will see them through the jaundiced spectacles provided by the corporate-owned media.

Trial lawyers should have their ears tuned to the frequency of the universe but what they usually hear is static.

~

~

Lawyers should be respectful of judges when the judge warrants respect, but do not ask me to respect a judge so brimming with prejudice or enmity he has forfeited his right to judge.

The courtroom is a breeding ground for lies and half-truths.

∽

Trials, Trial Lawyers and the Law

~

I think lawyers should respect each other, but do not ask me to respect a scheming, furtive scoundrel who cannot be trusted to play by the rules.

I think lawyers should respect the system, but do not ask me to respect a system that is unjust, that exploits the poor, that cowers to the rich and loves power and money over justice.

∽

Trials, Trial Lawyers and the Law

∼

Some judges are put off at the open process of an honest *voir dire* that can reveal prejudices to the enlightenment of both sides of the case. Some will be appreciative of the learning experience the jury is going through. Some will be relieved to see an attorney up there telling the truth and soliciting the truth from jurors. The magic mirror is at work: we're in touch with our feelings and our prejudices and we're being honest with the jurors. Their honesty has been reflected back. We've been open with them and their openness has been reflected back. It's that simple.

↜

Trials, Trial Lawyers and the Law

~

If truth and justice were persons they would shy away from the courtroom, for in the courtroom freakish fakes of truth and justice too often abound and flourish.

The law is a desert where human beings die thirsting for justice.

~

Trials, Trial Lawyers and the Law

~

A trial lawyer is a human being engaged in a life-changing struggle on behalf of other human beings.

Caring begets caring. Caring can change the dynamic in the courtroom.

Caring is contagious. It's a magical disease that can infect jurors.

Obstruction of justice is that catch-all crime that could convict a hen of sitting on her eggs.

~

No greater punishment exists than that imposed on the innocent.

Love is a stranger to the law.

~

~

Law is the father of injustice.

Mercy and the law are antagonists.

Trials, Trial Lawyers and the Law

~

The law makes its judgment like a young child playing with blocks. The block fits in the hole or not, and if not, the child rejects the block.

The law is a mindless weapon wielded in the hands of the powerful, usually against the powerless.

~

Ideas Worth Pondering

~

Most geniuses can't figure out how to tie their shoes.

Can we ever change at our core? Don't we recognize the unalterable difference in the temperament between a pit bull terrier and a spaniel?

~

Ideas Worth Pondering

~

I consider lectures as meat for the lecturer, but not much nourishment for the student.

Trends, fads, and schools of thought are the enemies of creativity.

Ideas Worth Pondering

~

Wisdom is only the aftermath of the diminishing testosterone levels in the aging male.

One walks up to the gaming table of life and throws the dice, and the winner is one who has made a fortunate draw of one's genes.

~

Ideas Worth Pondering

~

Some odorous guru with a yellowed beard said that success depends on the choices we make. I say that life is mostly in the power of luck—in the genes we drew. If that were not so, the guru would not have had the wherewithal to foist his dubious insight on us.

Ideas Worth Pondering

~

If man could rid himself of testosterone he could eliminate most crimes—crimes of jealousy, of the animal quest for dominance over the female, the money crimes that represent the male's push for power over other males, and the sort of crimes prevalent on Wall Street that are sex substitutes for the otherwise piteously impotent who jump and dance and lie to the music of dollars like idiots in a war dance around a bonfire of paper money.

~

Ideas Worth Pondering

~

Time is, after all, only a concept, and it finally dies with the death of any who seek to measure it.

For the rich, crime is often a money sport.

~

The Self

~

I know that love is worth the time it takes to find. Think of that when all the world seems made of walk-up rooms. And hands in empty pockets.

My highest self is like the elusive butterfly in a windstorm.

~

The Self

~

The child within never changes—it is only how we see the child that changes.

None of us live a toll-free life.

~

The Self

~

I will never live long enough to become a perfect fool. I must be satisfied with simply being the fool that I am.

Trying to find the self is like a worm trying to identify itself in a barrel of spaghetti.

~

The Self

~

I am a boatman on the river.

I am a child with many children.

The Self

~

Shame does not set well in the stomach and is hard to digest.

Everyone lies and everyone hates liars because everyone hates themselves for lying.

∽

The Self

~

Insanity itself is merely the product of the panicked mind seeking to affirm its own sanity as it is being judged by those who claim to be sane in an insane world.

I would rather not be a bumbler, but I must always retain my credibility even if, in doing so, I become a bumbler.

~

The Self

~

The true master is always the student.

~

The Self

~

Guilt, the self's most destructive weapon against the self.

We humans always interpret our conduct in ways that will relieve us of as much guilt as possible.

~

The Self

~

The human mind, with that gaping hole through which most of our lives have passed and left small, but often inaccurate traces on the edges, is something we call "memory."

Thank God for the merciful memory eraser known as time, although it never leaves a clean board, only a smeared one.

~

The Self

~

I tend to distrust those who shoot me a
hermetically sealed smile.

Facts

~

Facts are like a coloring book. The picture that comes out depends on who chooses the crayons.

∽

Freedom

~

Freedom is like an artist's blank, white canvas of the soul on which no commitments, no relationships, no plans, no values, no moral restraints have yet been painted.

Blind beliefs will hasten the end of a free people.

~

Freedom

~

Freedom is a tenant that occupies the house within.

Freedom is for sale only from the self.

Freedom

~

Perfect freedom is perfect nothingness.

Pure freedom is pure terror.

Freedom

~

Money censors the media.

The domestication of man and beast muffles the cry of freedom and suffocates the spirit of liberty.

Freedom

~

Freedom of the press, its sister, freedom of speech, and the firstborn, freedom of thought, are all children of Mother Liberty.

I would rather be unhealthy and free than a slave in good health.

~

Freedom

~

The cuisine of television entertainment we Americans are fed is to distract us from the servitude we endure and to occupy us so as not to overthrow our masters—the corporate glob.

Freedom—that which lies within.

Freedom

~

Once slavery in America was not seen as radical. It became, instead, a revolutionary idea that slaves should be freed. When we have lived under a pernicious power long enough, no matter how oppressive, we grow so accustomed to the yoke that its removal seems frightening, even wrong.

~

Freedom

~

Freedom cannot be given, except as we give it to ourselves.

Skepticism is the father of freedom. It is like the pry that holds the door open for truth to slip in.

Politicians and Government

~

Congress—a den of moral lepers who owe their souls to those who fill their begging bowls.

Congress—a pit one cannot enter without becoming diseased.

Politicians and Government

~

Government is operated by deeply embedded, hopelessly entangled bureaus where nothing is accomplished because the function of government is to intercept every living idea and smother it.

A politician: a stuffed horse's ass in chronic verbal flatulence.

~

Politicians and Government

～

Government is no longer the servant of the people but, at last, has become the people's master.

The difference we hear (between the political parties) is mostly the yapping of well-kept house dogs yapping at each other.

～

Democracy

~

Democracy—seemingly a fine form of government so long as the people do not engage in it.

Democracy—a form of government that exists chiefly as myth in the minds of the people.

〜

Democracy

~

Democracy, as practiced, has not succeeded in delivering democracy.

Democracy, as practiced in America, is that form of government that counts not ballots, but dollars.

～

Success

~

Success—in America, that malignant magic by which all that breathes, all that grows, all that is green is transformed into dead green money.

To freely bloom—that is my definition of success.

〜

Business

~

Free enterprise is free if you have enough money.

Free enterprise—an American religion.

Business

~

Corporate management is like a bird on the back of a galloping steed. The bird has little control of the horse, is there mostly for the ride, and can fly off whenever the horse stumbles and falls.

Profit—the ultimate moral imperative, the first and last commandment in American business.

～

Business

~

America's New King—the corporate core, the regime, the oligarchy that rules America, a conglomerate of none-living corporations. The New King is dead. It does not breathe.

~

Business

~

America has become a conglomeration of corporations like a new hatch of cutworms in the cabbage patch.

~

〜

Bank payments—our tribute of green flesh.

Business always trumps beauty.

᭝

Law Schools and Teaching

~

The best way to provide one's self a premature death is to attend law school from which you will matriculate as the walking dead.

You cannot teach what you cannot do. Too many professors have never tried a case.

~

Law Schools and Teaching

~

We can only teach people what they already know.

Our legal education is worse than the blind leading the blind. The blind care enough for the blind not to lead them.

~

Insurance Companies

~

The public at large insures the lives
of the insurance companies, not the
other way around.

Insurance Companies

~

I'd rather trust the Mafia for full, honest protection than an insurance company.

Argument

~

While birds can fly, and fish can live in the water, only humans can argue.

Argument is the affirmation of our being.

Argument

~

As a protest, argument struggles for justice, as a plea, it can generate mercy.

Charismatic oration moves multitudes and changes history—ask Lincoln, ask Franklin Roosevelt, ask Winston Churchill, ask Martin Luther King Jr.

෴

Argument

~

We must argue—to help, to warn, to lead, to love, to create, to learn, to achieve justice, to be.

One does not give away one's power by reacting to one's opponent. That puts one's opponent in charge.

~

Argument

When it comes to plain talk, lawyers are the worst. Most speak and write as if they live in a repository for dead bodies. When they write briefs that some poor trapped judge must read, they fill them with heavy, gray, lifeless, disgustingly boring word gravel—piles of it. When I read most briefs I want to scream. I want to throw the brief out the window and jump. If I could find the author, and had the power, I would make the villain eat the thing page at a time, without salt or catsup.

Argument

~

To move others we must first be moved.
To persuade others, we must first be
credible. To be credible, we must tell
the truth and the truth always begins
with feelings.

About Gerry Spence

Born, reared, and educated in Wyoming, Gerry Spence is recognized nationwide for his legacy of powerful courtroom victories and as the founder of the nationally acclaimed Trial Lawyers College, which established a revolutionary method for training lawyers to work for social justice. He has spent his career, both as an attorney and as a teacher of attorneys, striving on behalf of ordinary citizens.

He has received numerous awards including an Honorary Doctor of Laws degree from the University of Wyoming, and in 2009 was inducted into the American Trial Lawyers Hall of Fame. Gerry Spence is the author of eighteen other books, including the best-selling *How to Argue and Win Every Time* and the widely-acclaimed novel, *Half-Moon and Empty Stars*. He lives in Jackson Hole, Wyoming, with his wife of forty years, Imaging. They have six children and thirteen grandchildren.

The collected sayings in this volume, written over a span of fifty years, offer insightful windows into the life and passions of Gerry Spence, the man who would become one of the great American lawyers of our time.

Enjoy other Sastrugi Press Titles

50 Wildlife Hotspots by
Moose Henderson
   Find out where to find animals and photograph them in Grand Teton National Park from a professional wildlife photographer. Illustrated with maps.

A Small Pile of Feathers by
Gerry Spence
   Gerry Spence reveals his spiritual, loving, and sometimes humorous sides, depicted in his devotion to family and to preserving the wild places he writes of as though they were inscribed on his own bones and in his own blood.

Blood, Water, Wind, and Stone
edited by Lori Howe
Blood, Water, Wind, & Stone is a celebration of Wyoming and Wyoming writers. Experience the state through the vision of dozens of poets, nonfiction, and fiction writers.

Cache Creek by Susan Marsh

Five minutes from the hubbub of Jackson's town square, Cache Creek offers the chance for hikers to immerse themselves in wild nature. It is a popular hiking, biking, and cross-country ski area on the outskirts of Jackson, Wyoming.

Cloudshade by Lori Howe, Ph.D.

The poems of *Cloudshade* breathe with the vivid, fragrant essence of life in every season on America's high plains. Extraordinarily relatable, the poems of *Cloudshade* swing wide a door to life in the West, both for lovers of poetry and for those who rarely read poems.

Jackson Hole Hiking Guide by Aaron Linsdau

Find the best hiking trails in Jackson Hole. You'll get maps, GPS coordinates, accurate routes, elevation info, advantages, and dangers. The guide includes easy, challenging, family-friendly, and ADA-accessible trails and hikes.

Sleeping Dogs Don't Lie by
Michael McCoy
  A young Native American boy is taken from his home after tragedy strikes, grows up in middle America, and through his first real adult summer searches for Wyoming artifacts, and attempts single-handedly to solve the murder of his treasured coworker.

Voices at Twilight by Lori Howe, Ph.D.
  Voices at Twilight is a collection of poems, historical essays, and photographs that offers the reader a visual tour of twelve past and present Wyoming ghost towns.

Visit Sastrugi Press on the web to purchase the above titles in bulk. They are also available from your local bookstore or online retailers in print, e-book, or audiobook form.

www.sastrugipress.com
Thank you for choosing Sastrugi Press.
"Turn the Page Loose"

www.ingramcontent.com/pod-product-compliance
Lightning Source LLC
Chambersburg PA
CBHW060017050426
42448CB00012B/2789